Short Stories for Students, Volume 23

Project Editor: Anne Marie Hacht

Editorial: Sara Constantakis, Angela Doolin, Ira Mark Milne **Rights Acquisition and Management**: Lisa Kincade, Jackie Jones, and Kim Smilay **Manufacturing**: Drew Kalasky

Imaging and Multimedia: Lezlie Light, Mike Logusz, Kelly A. Quin **Product Design**: Pamela A. E. Galbreath **Vendor Administration**: Civie Green

Product Manager: Meggin Condino

For more information, contact
Gale, an imprint of Cengage Learning
27500 Drake Rd.
Farmington Hills, MI 48331-3535
Or you can visit our Internet site at

editors or publisher. Errors brought to the attention of the publisher and verified to the satisfaction of the publisher will be corrected in future editions.

ISBN 0-7876-7031-6
ISSN 1092-7735

Printed in the United States of America
10 9 8 7 6 5 4 3 2 1

Brokeback Mountain

Annie Proulx 1998

Introduction

Annie Proulx's short story "Brokeback Mountain" gained a great deal of attention before it was collected into her *Close Range: Wyoming Stories* in 1999. It was first published in the *New Yorker* in 1998 and subsequently won the magazine's award for fiction that year. It also appeared in the 1998 edition of *The O. Henry Stories*. Recognizing that it was the strongest story in her collection, Proulx placed it at the end of the book. When the reviews of *Close Range* appeared, "Brokeback Mountain" was consistently singled out for its evocative detail and compelling narrative.

The story chronicles the relationship between

Ennis del Mar and Jack Twist, two men who develop a deep love for each other but who are forced to live separate lives in an intolerant world. They meet as teenagers hired to herd sheep on Brokeback Mountain in Wyoming. Their quick friendship soon evolves into a strong sexual and emotional union—one that they fear may eventually cost them their lives. As Proulx traces the development of the love that grows between these two men and the forces that try to impede that love, she shapes the interplay of desire and denial into a heartbreaking story of loss and endurance.

Author Biography

Annie Proulx was born in Norwich, Connecticut, in 1935 to George and Lois Proulx. Her ancestors had lived in the area of Connecticut for over 350 years as farmers, artists, and mill workers. During Annie's youth, her father worked in the textile industry, so the family moved all over the country as he advanced his career. Annie attended high school in North Carolina and Maine; the family also spent time in Vermont and Rhode Island.

After graduating high school, Proulx attended the University of Vermont, where she received her bachelor of arts in 1969. She then attended graduate school in Montreal at Sir George Williams University where she received her master of arts in 1973.

Proulx's mother, Lois, was an artist and had a strong family tradition of oral story-telling. Many of her inventive ancestors could tell a story using everyday objects. This tradition helped to spawn Annie's interest in telling stories of her own. Proulx began writing initially to support her three children. She wrote mostly informational books that covered topics ranging from canoeing to African beadwork. During this period, she somehow found time to write fiction as well, which eventually was collected into *Heart Songs and Other Stories* in 1988.

After the success of this collection, her publisher persuaded her to write a novel. Her first,

Postcards (1992), is about the decline of the American farm family. *Postcards* won the PEN/Faulkner Award as well as rave reviews from publications such as the *New York Times.*

Proulx had another novel published the following year, *The Shipping News*, which won her even more critical acclaim as well as a Pulitzer Prize. This novel captured her love for Newfoundland's history, geography, and people. It illustrated the struggle between the harsh geography and climate of the region and its inhabitants.

Her next novel, *Accordion Crimes*, published in 1996, gained decent reviews, although not as strong as those for *The Shipping News* and *Postcards. Accordion Crimes* did, however, earn Proulx the Dos Passos Prize for literature.

After this novel, Proulx decided to go back to her first love, short-story writing. She prefers writing short stories to novels since she enjoys the challenges involved with making every word count. Her collection of short stories *Close Range: Wyoming Stories*, published in 1999, explores myths of the West, in which Proulx had been interested since she moved to Wyoming in 1995. The collection earned her overwhelmingly positive reviews. "Brokeback Mountain," the most critically acclaimed story in the collection, earned the *New Yorker* Award for fiction in 1998 and has been often anthologized, including in *The O. Henry Stories* published in 1998.

Plot Summary

Part 1

"Brokeback Mountain" begins in the present with Ennis Del Mar waking up in his trailer parked on the Wyoming ranch where he has been working. He thinks about finding a new job since the owner is ready to sell the ranch and acknowledges that he may have to live with his daughter for a while. This morning, though, he feels happy because he dreamed of Jack Twist the night before and of their time together on Brokeback Mountain.

At this point, the narrative shifts to 1983, when he and Jack were both teenagers during Ennis's first summer on the mountain where they worked as sheep herders. Day after day, Ennis tends the camp while Jack herds the sheep and sleeps out on the mountain with them. One day, when Jack complains about his "commutin four hours a day," he accepts Ennis's offer to switch jobs.

Every evening, they share supper by the campfire, "talking horses and rodeo, roughstock events, wrecks and injuries sustained," and other details of their hard lives in the West. Toward the end of the summer when they shift the camp, the distance Ennis has to ride out to the sheep grows longer and he begins to stay later at the camp at night. One evening, after the two sing drunken songs by the campfire, Ennis decides it is too late to go out to the sheep and so beds down at the campsite. After his shivering wakes Jack, the latter insists that Ennis share his bedroll. Soon after, the two have sex, something Ennis had never done before.

Their sexual activity becomes more frequent in the following days while they both insist that neither of them is "queer." One day the foreman, Joe Aguirre, watches them together through his binoculars. Toward the end of the summer, after Ennis spends an entire night with Jack, the sheep wander off and mix with another group of sheep. Ennis tries unsuccessfully to sort them out. When they come down off the mountain after the first snowfall, Aguirre notes with displeasure that the sheep count is low and the herd is mixed.

When Jack asks Ennis if he is coming back to the mountain the next summer, Ennis tells him that he will be getting married in December and then will try to find work on a ranch. Jack determines to go back home and then maybe to Texas, and the two say an awkward goodbye. As Ennis drives away, his gut wrenches and he retches along the side of the road. He feels "about as bad as he ever had," a feeling that stays with him for a long time.

Part 2

Ennis marries Alma and a year later their child is born. After the ranch where he was working folds, he reluctantly takes work on a road crew. When their second child is born, Alma convinces him to get a place in town so that she will not have to live on any more "lonesome ranches."

Four summers after their first on Brokeback Mountain, Jack visits Ennis. When Jack first arrives, he and Ennis share a passionate embrace, watched by Alma. When Jack meets Alma, he announces that he too is married and has one child. After a few awkward moments, Ennis and Jack leave, pick up a bottle of whiskey and head for a motel where they spend the night together.

They talk of how they missed each other and of Jack's career as a bull rider. Jack suggests that he married his wife, Lureen, because she came from a wealthy family. Ennis admits that he has been thinking about whether he is gay but insists that he is not. He explains that he does not enjoy sex with women, but he has not been with any other man. Jack declares the same. After the two express their passion for each other, Jack notes, "we got us a f— situation here. Got a figure out what to do." Ennis determines that nothing can be done since they both have families and warns Jack that if they are seen together, they may be killed.

Jack informs Ennis that he thinks someone saw them together on the mountain, but does not tell him that it was Aguirre, who subsequently did not rehire Jack for the ranch. When Jack insists the two could get a ranch together, Ennis declares that he is stuck in his situation and cannot get out. He does not want to end up like a gay man in his hometown who was beaten to death by the locals. His father, who had taken him to see the corpse, would have, Ennis insists, done the same to him if he had walked into their motel room. The only future Ennis can see for the two of them is to get together once in a while, explaining "if you can't fix it you got to stand it." Despondent, Jack convinces Ennis to go with him for a few days into the mountains.

Media Adaptations

"Brokeback Mountain" was made into an award-winning film, starring Heath Ledger and Jake Gyllenhaal. Directed by Ang Lee, the film was released in 2005

Part 3

Ennis and Alma grow apart as she begins to resent him for not finding a steady, well-paying job and for his occasional fishing trips with Jack. When she eventually divorces him, he returns to ranch work. He stays in touch with Alma, who has remarried, and with his children. One night when he visits them, Alma tells him that she knows that he and Jack never did any fishing on their trips together. When she voices her disgust over his relationship with Jack, Ennis physically threatens her and storms out to a bar where he picks a fight.

During the following years, Ennis and Jack occasionally meet on different ranges throughout the West. One night, they catch each other up on their lives, both admitting affairs with women and problems with their own children. After complaining about the infrequency of their time together, Jack suggests that they move to Mexico, but Ennis declines, insisting that he has to stay and work. When Ennis expresses his pain over their separation, Jack reminds him that Ennis turned down a life together and declares that he can barely stand being apart from Ennis. Overwhelmed with emotion, Ennis drops to his knees. Later, Jack remembers a perfect moment of togetherness on Brokeback Mountain.

Part 4

Months later, when Ennis receives back a postcard he had sent to Jack marked "DECEASED," he calls Lureen, who informs him that Jack was killed when a tire blew up in his face. Ennis suspects, however, that he was murdered after he was caught with another man. He makes a trip to see Jack's parents and offers to take Jack's ashes up to Brokeback Mountain, where Jack had told

Lureen that he wanted to be buried.

Jack's father admits that Jack had planned on bringing Ennis up to his family's ranch to work it with him. When Jack's father tells Ennis that not too long ago, Jack found another man that he wanted to bring to the ranch, Ennis realizes that Jack was murdered. As he notes Mr. Twist's coldness, Ennis remembers Jack telling him about a vicious beating he received from his father when he was a small child.

During the visit, Ennis goes up to Jack's room where he finds Jack's shirt, which is covered in Ennis's blood. He remembers Jack accidentally kneeing his nose during lovemaking on the mountain. Inside the shirt, he finds one of his own. Ennis then buries his face in Jack's shirt, hoping to be able to smell his scent, but there is nothing there. Before Ennis leaves, Mr. Twist informs him that Jack's ashes will be buried in the family plot, what Ennis calls that "grieving plain," instead of on the mountain.

The narrative then jumps back to the beginning of the story as Ennis orders a postcard of Brokeback Mountain in the local store. When it arrives, he pins it up in his trailer above the two shirts from Jack's room hung on a hanger. During that time, a young Jack appears in his dreams along with visions of their time at Brokeback Mountain, which would fill him sometimes with grief, sometimes with joy. The story ends with what has become Ennis's motto: "if you can't fix it you've got to stand it."

Characters

Joe Aguirre

Joe Aguirre, the foreman of the ranch that hires Ennis and Jack to herd sheep on Brokeback Mountain, considers the two to be a "[p]air of deuces going nowhere." He spies on them through binoculars, watching their lovemaking. His disgust over their homosexuality prompts him to refuse to rehire Jack the following summer. Joe's attitude foreshadows the prejudice the two will encounter as they continue their relationship.

Alma Del Mar

Alma Del Mar is present to show Ennis's failure to adopt a conventional heterosexual life. She adds to Ennis's sense of shame with "her misery voice" and her growing resentment over his relationship with Jack and his emotional distance from her and their children.

Ennis Del Mar

Nineteen-year-old Ennis Del Mar accepts a herding job on Brokeback Mountain in Wyoming so that he can earn enough money to marry Alma Beers. He was forced to drop out of high school after his parents died and now has no other prospects. He was brought up, though, "to hard work and privation," and "inured to the stoic life." This stoicism helps him endure the pain of Jack's death.

Up on the mountain, he begins a passionate yet limited relationship with Jack Twist. When Jack initiates their first sexual encounter, Ennis immediately responds since he "ran full-throttle on all roads whether fence mending or money spending." While on the mountain, Ennis feels that he and Jack "*owned the world and nothing seemed wrong.*" yet he ultimately is unable to accept his homosexuality, insisting that he is "no queer." Ennis continually tries to deny his feelings, at one point telling Jack "I like doin it with women" and "I never had no thoughts a doin it with another guy." Yet the fact that he prefers anal sex with Alma suggests the true nature of his sexuality.

Ennis struggles to follow the conventional path, marrying Alma and raising a family, but he cannot completely repress his passion for Jack. He is unable to establish a sense of permanence with Alma, continually choosing unfulfilling jobs and small apartments that "could be left at any time." Eventually, his emotional distance from Alma breaks up their marriage.

Ennis's shame over his sexual orientation makes it difficult for him to embrace Jack face to face. It also sometimes prompts violent outbursts. His father had taught him to solve problems with his fists when Ennis's older brother kept beating him up. This streak emerges when Alma voices her disgust over his relationship with Jack and in a jealous response to Jack's suggestion that he has been with other men in Mexico. Ennis warns him, "all them things I don't know could get you killed if I should come to know them."

Ennis's internalized homophobia and stoicism allow him to endure the long separations from Jack and Jack's death. He spends his final years alone, dreaming of his time with Jack on Brokeback Mountain.

Mr. Del Mar

Ennis's father, Mr. Del Mar, epitomizes the intolerant world that Ennis and Jack must face. Even though he never appears in the story, he has a strong impact on his son. His response to the murder of a homosexual man fills Ennis with shame and fear when his own homosexual longings emerge.

Jack Twist

Jack Twist comes to Brokeback Mountain because he is "crazy to be somewhere, anywhere else than Lightning Flat" where he grew up. Jack is able to express more freely his homosexuality, admitting that he never wanted a family. He engages in sexual relations with other men after he and Ennis leave Brokeback Mountain, which eventually gets him killed.

Since he conveys no sense of shame over his

homosexuality, he has an easier time expressing his love for Ennis. He continually notes the magnitude of their feelings for each other, at one point insisting, "[t]his ain't no little thing that's happenin here." When Ennis refuses to spend more time with him, Jack becomes bitter and impatient. He recognizes the truth about their relationship in a way that Ennis cannot, noting that Ennis keeps him on a "short leash." Jack admits that his overwhelming, frustrated desire for Ennis has caused him to turn to other men. Yet Jack's deep love for him, which is not openly returned, causes him to declare to Ennis, "I wish I knew how to quit you."

Jack expresses the depth of his feeling for Ennis with his memory of a perfect moment they shared on the mountain. One day, Ennis had come up behind him and held him for a long time. That embrace became for him "the single moment of artless, charmed happiness in their separate and difficult lives." He longs to experience more of such moments with Ennis "in a way he could neither help nor understand."

Jack's lack of shame over his sexual orientation causes him to take too many chances in the intolerant world in which he lives. While his wife Lureen claims that Jack died when a tire he was fixing exploded in his face, Ennis understands that Jack was beaten to death, just like the homosexual man had been who lived in the town where Ennis grew up.

Lureen Twist

Jack marries Lureen because her family has money. She appears briefly in the story as a plot device in order to give Jack some financial options and to provide a conventional façade for him.

Mr. Twist

Mr. Twist is the embodiment of the masculine Western stereotype. Ennis recognizes his need to be "the stud duck in the pond" when he visits him after Jack's death. Mr. Twist displayed his cruelty when he beat Jack for his accidents in the bathroom and his insensitivity when he refuses to let Ennis take Jack's ashes to Brokeback Mountain.

Intolerance

The concept of masculinity in the American West does not include homosexuality. Western legends, in literature and film, glorify men who display courage in the face of overwhelming odds and who as pairs ride off together into the sunset or as individuals return to women waiting patiently in the schoolhouse or in the farmhouse. These mythic stereotypes reflect a predominantly conservative set of values in the American West that refuses to recognize as natural a sexual union between two men. Proulx placed her protagonists in this intolerant setting and traces the suffering they experience as a result.

From an early age both Ennis and Jack are taught harsh lessons on how to act like a man. Mr. Twist would not tolerate four-year-old Jack's accidents in the bathroom, especially one night when he flew into a rage and whipped him with his belt. The young Jack was forced to endure the abuse of his father urinating on him so that he would understand the proper way for a man to relieve himself.

Mr. Del Mar's hatred of homosexuals caused him to force his son to look at a man who had been beaten to death because he had dared to love another man. Ennis wonders whether his father was the murderer but is certain that if he ever discovered his son with Jack, he would kill him. Ennis and Jack understand that homosexuality "don't happen in Wyomin" and if it does, those involved soon flee or die.

The training Ennis and Jack received when they were children makes them wary of openly expressing their love for each other. Ennis is more wary than Jack, who takes too many chances and, as a result, ends up being beaten to death with a tire iron, much like the man Ennis had seen when he was young. Ennis's fear of a violent confrontation causes him to deny the intensity of his feelings for Jack and to reject Jack's offers to live together. Ennis's fears are reinforced by his wife's response to his relationship with Jack. While she tolerates her husband's homosexual tendencies for a while, she ultimately cannot cope with his emotional distance. She finally confronts him with her knowledge of what the two really did on their "fishing trips" together and calls him, "Jack Nasty."

Shame

Ennis's internalization of the belief that homosexuality is indecent and punishable by death causes him to be ashamed about the intensity of his feelings for Jack. At the beginning of their relationship on the mountain, he insists that he is not "queer," that their feelings for each other are not indicative of his sexual orientation.

His shame, coupled with his need to maintain

the façade of his marriage in the face of public scrutiny, causes him to lie continually to Alma about his feelings for Jack, insisting that when she catches the two in a heated embrace, their actions are a result of their not having seen each other for four years. He also must deceive her each time he goes off with Jack, claiming that the two are on fishing trips. Alma discovers that he and Jack never actually fish on these trips when she tapes a note to his unused fishing rod.

His internalized homophobia makes him unable to accept himself or act congruently. This shame thus prevents him from escaping with Jack to a possibly more tolerant location, such as Mexico. Ennis needs to maintain the illusion of a conventional life, even if that life denies him the one person he desires most. Jack notes that as a result, all that they have left is their time on Brokeback Mountain, which Ennis thinks cast a spell on him, a belief that makes it easier for him to deal with his love for Jack.

Topics for Further Study

- Read two other short stories in Proulx's *Close Range* and write an essay comparing and contrasting the main themes.

- Watch the film version of the story and prepare a classroom presentation using clips from the film that analyzes how the filmmaker translated the text to the screen.

- Investigate the measures being taken to combat hate crimes against homosexuals. Write an essay discussing the measures and their effectiveness.

- Write a short story or poem with the title "If You Can't Fix It You've Got to Stand It" that focuses on the subject of loss or on the internal dilemma one feels in enduring a situation which cannot be fixed.

Style

Setting as Symbol

Proulx uses setting details to heighten the thematic significance of the story. The most effective use of setting as symbol occurs when she juxtaposes harsh and beautiful images of the landscape's cruel beauty to suggest the difficult nature of Ennis's and Jack's relationship. Proulx presents this juxtaposition first when Ennis and Jack initially herd the sheep up to Brokeback Mountain. The narrator likens the sheep's movement up the trail to the flow of "dirty water through the timber and out above the tree line into the great flowery meadows and the coursing, endless wind." The contrast between the dirty sheep and the meadow flowers seems to foreshadow the love that will grow between the two men as well as the prejudice their relationship will inspire.

This foreshadowing is reinforced when Proulx juxtaposes the "sweetened" cold air of the mountain on their first morning with the phallic "rearing lodgepole pines ... massed in slabs of somber malachite." When Ennis and Jack begin their sexual relationship, Proulx captures its harsh and exhilarating duality when she describes Jack and Ennis as "flying in the euphoric, bitter air" on the mountain.

After Jack dies, the landscape is filled with

bleakness, containing no moments of beauty that can relieve Ennis's heartache. Then "the huge sadness of the northern plains rolled down on him" as he passes "desolate country" with "houses sitting blank-eyed in the weeds." Although he tries to convince Jack's father to let him take Jack's ashes up to Brokeback Mountain, the old man refuses, committing them instead to "the grieving plain" that echoes Ennis's suffering.

Stories of the American West

Stories about the American West gained attention in the mid-nineteenth century and remained a popular genre during the first part of the twentieth century. The early Westerns followed a formulaic, stereotypical pattern: the main characters were mythic heroes that represented the American spirit of self-reliance and courage. The world of the Western was dominated by men; women were relegated to lesser roles, either as titillating saloon prostitutes or virginal schoolmarms and motherly farm women. Settings were picturesque and plots melodramatic, with scenes of violence often interspersed with humor.

The most popular fiction focused on cowboys who emerged in dime novels at the end of the nineteenth century and stories in magazines such as *Atlantic, Harpers*, and *Scribner's*. Some of the most popular writers in this genre were Alfred Henry Lewis, Henry Wallace Phillips, William R. Lighton, Rex Beach, and O. Henry, who set some of his stories in Texas. Perhaps the most famous and acclaimed Western is Zane Grey's *Riders of the Purple Sage*, published in 1912.

Western stories lost popularity in the second half of the twentieth century when war heroes and hardboiled detectives took the cowboy's place. In the 1960s, writers began to break out of the confines of traditional subject and technique and gained new audiences who responded to narratives that focused on anti-heroes, such as those in Thomas Berger's *Little Big Man* (1964) and E. L. Doctorow's *Welcome to Hard Times* (1975), and minority cultures, as those found in the work of N. Scott Momaday, Maxine Hong Kingston, Simon Ortiz, and Leslie Silko.

Discrimination against Homosexuals

Although Congress has made it a crime to discriminate against anyone based on his/her race, religion, sex, or national origin, as of 2006 it has not recognized the same rights for homosexuals. Some states, however, including Connecticut, Hawaii, Massachusetts, New Jersey, and Wisconsin, have outlawed discrimination on the basis of sexual orientation. Sodomy statutes, which typically call for a three-month jail sentence and fine, are still on the books in many (predominantly southern) states.

Discrimination in the education system is supported in states such as Oklahoma and West Virginia where school boards are mandated by law to fire homosexual teachers. High school and college students in many states across the country find it difficult to organize gay and lesbian student organizations. Homosexuals have been blocked from participation in those occupations which involve children.

The government practices discrimination in the military and positions that require top secret security clearances. In 1993, President Clinton tried to end this discrimination with the "Don't Ask, Don't Tell, Don't Pursue" policy, which stated that military personnel would not be asked questions about their sexual orientation. Yet harassment and discrimination continue for anyone in the military who is openly gay or suspected of being so. The military has determined that homosexuals cannot have successful careers in any of its branches and so discharges approximately one hundred servicemen and women each year who have admitted to being gay. Security clearances are denied homosexuals under the presumption that they may become blackmail targets by ex-lovers.

In states that do not recognize the rights of homosexuals, housing can be refused by landlords and homeowners. While California, Connecticut, the District of Columbia, Hawaii, Maine, New Jersey, and Vermont do not as of 2006 recognize same-sex unions, they do grant beneficiary rights to partners in these long-term relationships. Same sex marriage, along with adoption rights, is recognized by several countries including Denmark, Sweden, and Canada.

Anti-gay attitudes in the United States have led to an increase in hate crimes against homosexuals. This issue attracted national attention after the murder of Matthew Shepard, a homosexual student at the University of Wyoming, in 1998.

Critical Overview

The response to *Close Range: Wyoming Stories* and especially "Brokeback Mountain" was overwhelmingly positive. Dean Bakopoulos, in *The Progressive*, considers *Close Range* a "well-crafted collection" claiming, "this is powerful fiction, and somehow Proulx manages to give each story the plot, depth of character, sense of setting, and thematic weight of an entire novel." Rita D. Jacobs in an article for *World Literature Today* praises the collection's "luscious prose" and "evocative descriptions" that make "a strong impression" on the reader.

A reviewer for *Publishers Weekly* considers the book a "breathtaking compilation of Proulx's short fiction" that contains "an amazing, exhilarating range of mood, atmosphere and theme. Every one boasts prose that is smart, lively and fused with laconic poetry" and "her dexterity with striking images creates delights on every page." The reviewer claims that her stories are "focused by an immaculate eye and ear" and "every detail rings true" and finds a "stringent authority in her meticulous descriptions." The "distinctive impact" of Proulx's stories, the reviewer claims, is created through her "empathetic observations of the harsh conditions of her characters' lives" and "her grim awareness of the deadly accidents that can strike like lightning in the midst of exhausting daily routine."

Bakopoulos finds fault, however, with the pace of some of the stories, arguing that "on occasion, she packs in too much detail" especially in her openings. He concludes that "while impressive, this background information often slows the stories down." Jacobs insists that the stories are "uneven, but when they work, they are wondrous, with characters so alive and touching that the reader feels the ache of loss as the final page is turned."

Reviewers' highest praise is reserved for "Brokeback Mountain," which Bakopoulos calls "a tender and heartbreaking love story." He claims that its "crushing last line ... sums up all the loneliness and failed dreams that make *Close Range* such a moving and wise collection." The *Publishers Weekly* review also singles out the last line of the story, noting that in its "restrained but achingly tender narrative of forbidden love" Proulx merges "the matter-of-fact and the macabre, and her summary of life's pain in a terse closing sentence, will elicit gasps of pain and understanding." Jacobs argues that "Brokeback Mountain" is the collection's "most successful" story. She concludes, "In choosing such an unlikely setting for heartbreak and creating such strongly evocative settings and characters, Proulx proves her exquisite command of the story genre."

What Do I Read Next?

- *All the Pretty Horses* (1992), by Cormac McCarthy, focuses on the coming of age of its two protagonists in the Southwest and Mexico.

- Larry McMurtry's novel *Lonesome Dove* (1985) weaves together stories of cattle herding that portray the difficult lives men and women experienced in the American West at the end of the nineteenth century.

- Proulx's "The Half-Skinned Steer" (1998) appears in the same collection as "Brokeback Mountain" and focuses on the hard landscapes of the West and the troubled people who live there.

- *American West* (1994), by Dee

Brown, explores the last half of the nineteenth century and the development of the enduring myths of the West.

Sources

Bakopoulos, Dean, "Woes of the West," in the *Progressive* September 1999, pp. 43-44.

Jacobs, Rita D., Review of *Close Range: Wyoming Stories*, in *World Literature Today*, Vol. 74, No. 2, Spring 2000, p. 369.

Proulx, Annie, "Brokeback Mountain," in *Close Range: Wyoming Stories*, Scribner, 1999, pp. 255-85.

Review of *Close Range: Wyoming Stories*, in *Publishers Weekly*, March 29, 1999, p. 91.

Further Reading

Kowalewski, Michael, "Losing Our Place: A Review Essay," in *Michigan Quarterly Review*, Vol 40, No. 1, Winter 2001, pp. 242-57.

> This essay explores the sense of place in American fiction, including *Close Range*.

McGraw, Erin, "Brute Force: Violent Stories," in *Georgia Review*, Vol. 54, No. 2, Winter 2000, p. 351.

> McGraw traces the theme of violence in American fiction and compares the stories in *Close Range* to that tradition.

McMurtry, Larry, ed., *Still Wild: Short Fiction of the American West 1950 to the Present*, Simon and Shuster, 2001.

> This collection includes stories by Richard Ford, Raymond Carver, Leslie Marmon Silko, and Jack Kerouac.

Steinberg, Sybil, "E. Annie Proulx: An American Odyssey," in *Publishers Weekly*, June 3, 1996, pp. 57-58.

> Steinberg focuses on Proulx's life and work in this overview.

9 781375 377638